THE NATURE KIDS GUIDE TO

REINDEER

DAVID ANDERSON

LP Media Inc. Publishing
Text copyright © 2026 by LP Media Inc.
All rights reserved.

For information address LP Media Inc. Publishing,
30012 Variolite St NW, Princeton MN 55371
www.lpmedia.org

Publication Data

Reindeer
The Nature Kid's Guide to Reindeer — First edition.

Summary: "Learn all about Reindeer, the Nature Kid Way"
— Provided by publisher.

ISBN: 979-8-89818-111-6

[1. Reindeer – Non-Fiction] I. Title.

Title: The Nature Kid's Guide to Reindeer

CONTENTS

FROZEN FRONTIER

DID YOU KNOW?

Reindeer and Caribou are the same animal. The name changes depending on where you live. In Europe they call them Reindeer, while North Americans use Caribou!

4

Crunch! A reindeer walks on frozen snow. Its wide hooves grip the ice.

Reindeer live in frozen lands. Snow covers the ground for many months. They live in some of the coldest places on Earth.

Winters are long and dark. The sun does not rise for weeks. Summers are short but bright. Some summer days the sun never sets.

Reindeer need open **tundra** to find food. Tundra is flat land with no trees. The ground stays frozen under the surface. Some reindeer also live in cold forests.

Reindeer are built for this icy world. Their bodies help them survive the bitter cold.

ARCTIC ADDRESS

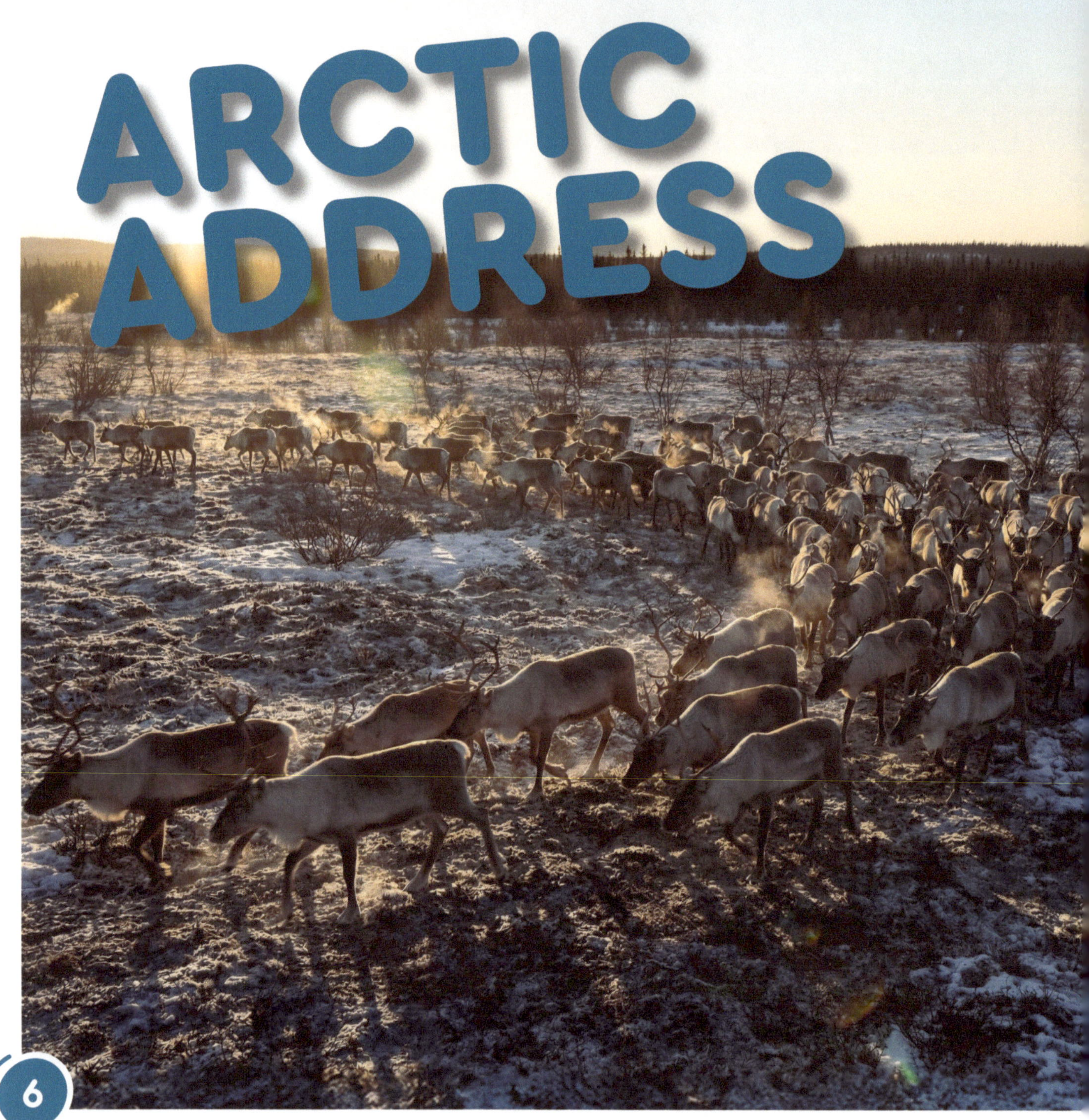

Stomp! A reindeer herd crosses the tundra together.

Reindeer live in northern cold countries like Norway, Sweden, and Finland. They also live in Russia.

Alaska and Canada have Reindeer too, but they call them Caribou. Even Greenland has Reindeer living there!

The Svalbard reindeer live only on islands near Norway. They are much smaller than their mainland cousins!

Reindeer can smell lichen buried under three feet of snow to find their food.

BIG BUDDIES

Snort! A big reindeer stands next to a smaller one.

Reindeer come in different sizes. Males are called bulls, and they are bigger than females. Bulls can weigh up to 700 pounds.

Females are called cows. They usually weigh around 300 pounds. That is less than half the size of a bull!

Calves are born small, weighing about 13 pounds at birth. They grow fast on their mother's rich milk.

Newborn reindeer calves can stand and walk within one hour of being born.

RADICAL RACKS

Crack! A reindeer shakes its big antlers. Velvet hangs off.

Reindeer have amazing antlers. Both males and females grow them. This makes reindeer special. They are the only deer species where this happens.

Antlers are made of bone that grows from the top of the head. New antlers are covered in soft skin called velvet. Blood flows through this velvet to help antlers grow.

Antlers can grow very fast. Some bulls grow antlers over four feet wide!

Reindeer antlers grow about half an inch per day: one of nature's fastest tissues!

SUPER
SNIFFERS

Sniff! A reindeer lifts its nose high in the cold air.

Reindeer have a great sense of smell. Their noses help them survive in cold Arctic winters.

They can smell food under deep snow. This helps them find lichen and plants to eat.

Reindeer use smell to find their herd. Mothers and calves know each other by scent. Smell helps keep families together.

Inside a reindeer's nose is a shape like a seashell. This swirly shape gives the nose a huge surface area to warm cold air super fast.

13

BUILT TOUGH

Thump! A reindeer kicks at the hard, frozen ground. It searches for food.

Reindeer have bodies built for cold weather. Their thick fur has two layers. The outer layer has hollow hairs that trap warm air inside.

Their noses warm cold air before it reaches their lungs. Special blood vessels inside the nose heat the air as reindeer breathe in.

Reindeer hooves change with the seasons. In summer, soft pads help them walk on wet ground. In winter, the soft pads shrink and hard edges pop out to grip the ice.

Reindeer fur traps heat so well that snow landing on them doesn't even melt!

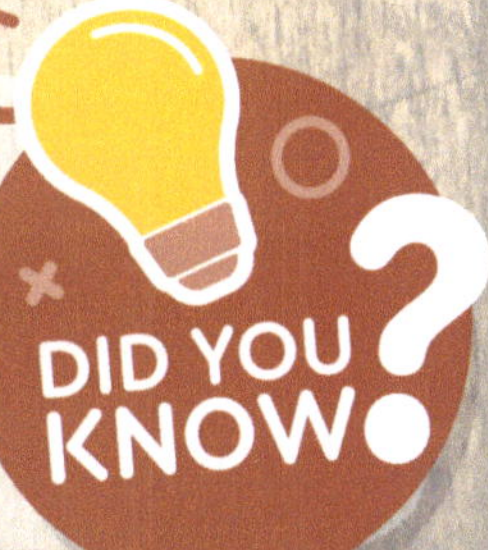

15

LICHEN LUNCH

Chomp! A reindeer munches on fuzzy lichen. It chews each bite slowly.

Reindeer eat many different plants. Their diet changes with the seasons.

In summer, they eat grasses, leaves, and mushrooms. These green plants give them lots of energy.

In winter, food is harder to find. Reindeer eat **lichen** that grows on rocks and trees. Lichen is not a plant. It is a mix of fungus and algae. This special food helps reindeer survive.

Reindeer can eat up to 18 pounds of food a day during the summer months!

REINDEER CHATTER

Reindeer knees make clicking sounds when they walk. Herds can hear each other!

Click! A reindeer makes a sound with its knees.

Reindeer talk to each other in many ways. They make grunting sounds. Mothers and babies call back and forth. This helps them find each other in large herds.

Reindeer also use their bodies to communicate. They hold their heads high to look big. They lower their antlers as a warning. Other reindeer understand these signs.

Smell is important too. Reindeer have scent glands near their eyes. They leave their smell on trees and bushes. This tells other reindeer they were there.

WATCH OUT

Howl! A wolf pack spots a reindeer herd. The reindeer lift their heads.

Reindeer face many **predators**. Wolves hunt reindeer in packs. They chase herds across the tundra.

Brown bears also hunt reindeer. Bears often catch young calves in spring. Golden eagles are dangerous too. They swoop down and attack small calves with sharp talons.

Wolverines are fierce hunters as well. These strong animals can even take down reindeer alone. Reindeer must always watch for danger.

DID YOU KNOW?

Even Lynx hunt reindeer calves in forests. They hide in trees and pounce.

21

RUN FAST

Whoosh! A reindeer sprints across open tundra. Its legs blur with speed.

Reindeer are fast runners. They can reach speeds up to 50 miles per hour. This helps them escape predators.

When danger comes, reindeer run together as a herd. Running in a group makes it harder for predators to catch one animal.

Calves can run soon after birth. Within one day, a calf keeps up with its mother.

Reindeer can also swim across wide rivers. They paddle with their legs and float well.

TREKKING TROTTERS

Click! A reindeer's ankle tendons snap with each step.

Reindeer are great travelers. They walk farther than almost any other land animal. Some herds travel over 3,000 miles each year.

Reindeer **migrate** with the seasons. They move north in summer and south in winter.

Reindeer can walk through deep snow. Their wide hooves spread out like snowshoes. This keeps them from sinking.

Reindeer ankles make a clicking sound when they walk! This helps the herd stay together in snowstorms when they can't see each other.

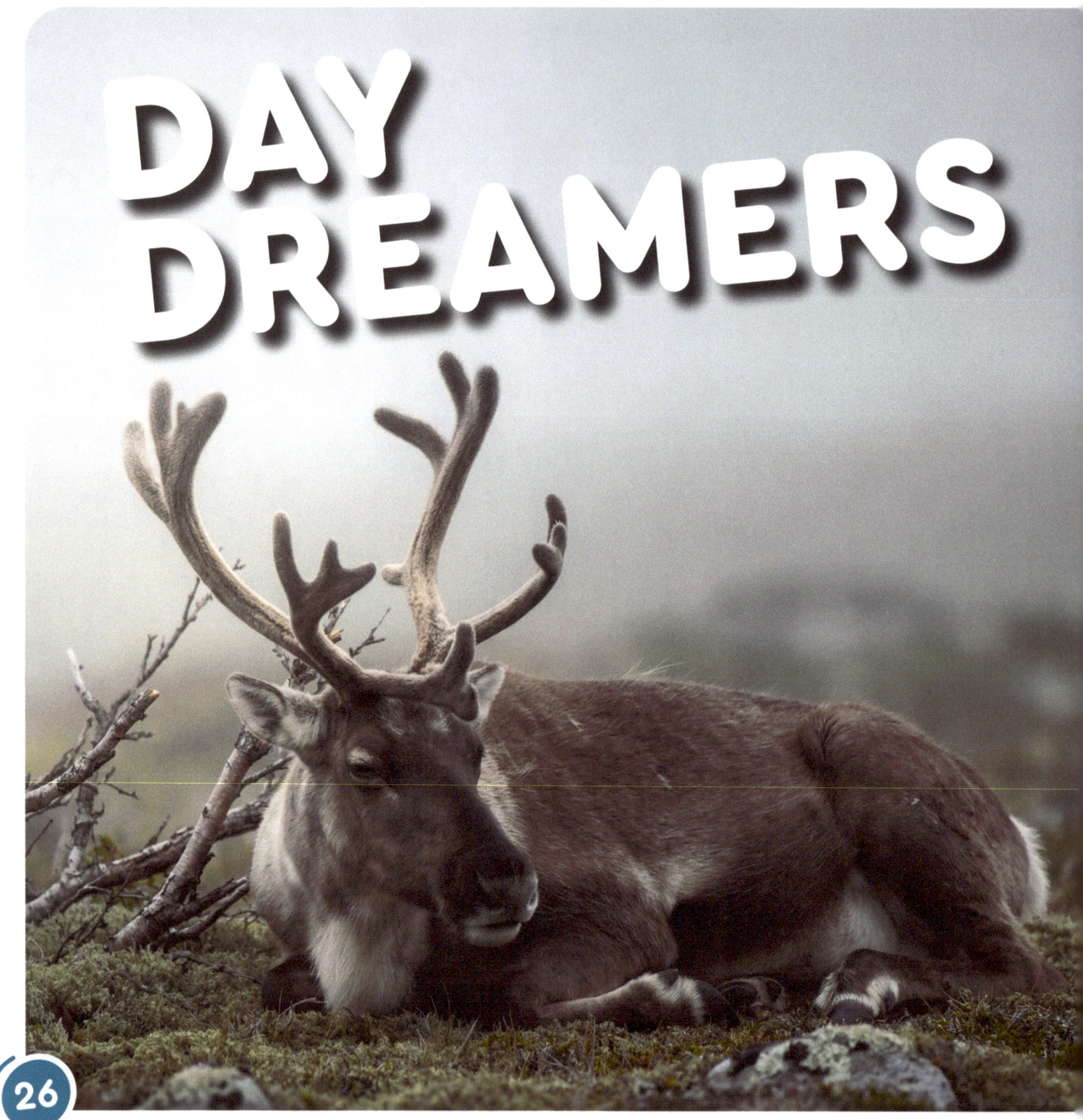

DAY DREAMERS

Grunt! A reindeer rests on soft moss. Its eyes slowly close.

Reindeer are active at all different times. They do not follow day and night like other animals.

Reindeer eat and rest in short bursts. They may graze for a few hours. Then they lie down. This happens all day and night.

In the Arctic, summer has constant sunlight. Winter brings long darkness. Reindeer adapt to both. They stay active when they need food.

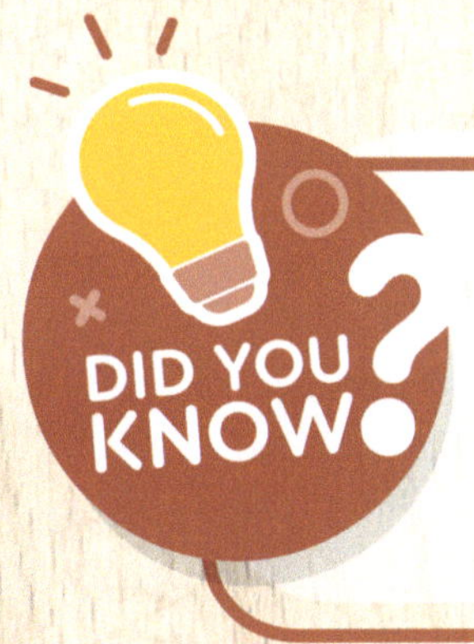

Reindeer eyes change color! They are golden in summer and blue in winter to see in darkness.

HERD HANGOUT

Rumble! Hundreds of reindeer move together. Their hooves pound the ground.

Reindeer live in large groups called herds. Some herds have thousands of animals. Living together helps keep them safe.

Herds are not quiet places. Reindeer make sounds to stay connected. Mothers and calves call to find each other.

Herds change size during the year. They grow larger when it is time to migrate.

Reindeer know each herd member by smell and voice. Each one has a unique call.

ANTLER ACTION

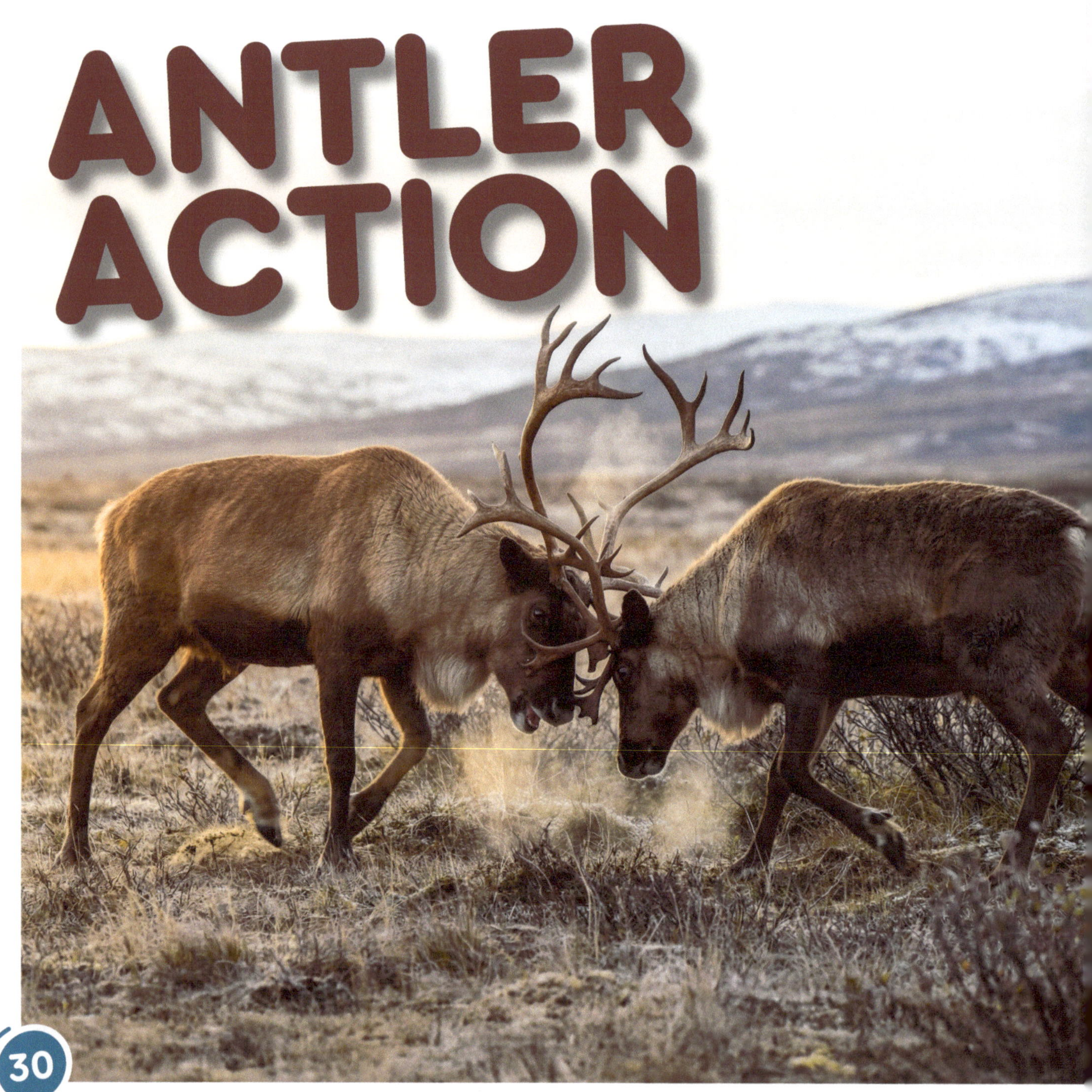

Snarl! Two male reindeer lower their antlers. They push hard.

Male reindeer compete each fall. They use their antlers to push and shove. The strongest males win these contests.

Males grow their biggest antlers for this season. Their necks get thick and strong too, which helps them push harder.

Female reindeer watch these contests nearby. They choose the winners as mates. Calves are then born the following spring in May or June.

Male reindeer can lose up to 30 percent of their body weight during the fall mating season.

CUTE CALVES

DID YOU KNOW?
Reindeer calves gain about one pound per day in their first month, making them fast-growing Arctic babies.

Squeak! A tiny reindeer calf stands on wobbly legs.

Baby reindeer are called calves. They are born in spring when the snow melts. These newborns have soft brown fur.

Calves can stand within one hour of birth. They start walking right away too. This helps them keep up with the moving herd.

Calves drink their mother's milk for the first few months. This rich food helps them grow fast. By fall, they eat plants like adult reindeer.

MOM KNOWS

Neigh! A mother reindeer nuzzles her calf gently in the snow.

Mother reindeer care for their calves alone. Fathers do not help. Moms do all the work.

Mothers and calves stay close. They know each other by smell. They know each other by sound. Each pair has a special call.

Mothers keep their calves safe. They use their antlers to fight off predators. Female reindeer are the only female deer with antlers. This makes them very fierce protectors.

Reindeer milk has over 20% fat to help calves grow fast and strong!

REMARKABLE
REINDEER

Click! A reindeer's hooves make sounds on ice.

Reindeer have adapted to live in cold places. Their special noses warm cold air before it reaches their lungs. This helps them breathe in freezing weather.

Reindeer hooves spread wide like snowshoes. This helps them walk on soft snow without sinking in.

They are like special Arctic superheroes!

Reindeer can see ultraviolet light. This helps them spot food and predators against the white snow that humans cannot see.

REINDEER HERDERS

Crunch! A reindeer herd walks through deep snow.

Some **nomadic** people called "herders" raise reindeer. They travel with their herds across the land. They check on them every day. They look for signs of sickness and injuries.

Reindeer need space to roam and graze. They eat grasses and mosses. They eat lichens too. Fresh water is important for them.

In winter, reindeer need extra help. Snow can cover their food. Herders move them to new areas.

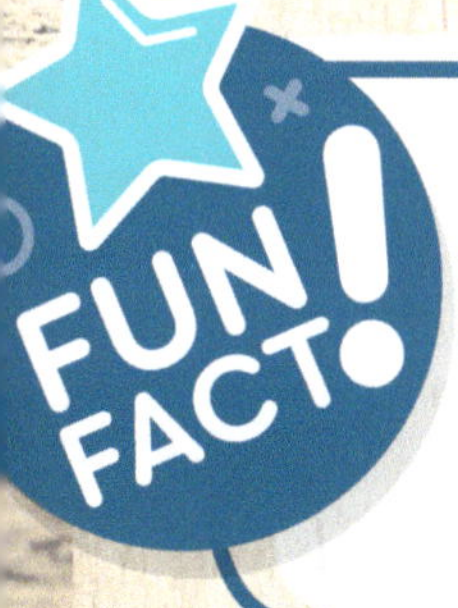

Reindeer herders in some regions use special ear markings to identify each animal.

GLOSSARY

lichen
A crusty living thing that grows on rocks and trees and is food for reindeer.

tundra
A flat, cold land where no trees grow and the ground stays frozen.

predators
Animals that hunt and eat other animals.

migrate
To travel a long way from one place to another when seasons change.

nomadic
Moving from place to place instead of staying in one home.